"There are some lines in the poem "Particles" that serve as a description for this lovely collection, taken as a whole: "think past particles/and fractal spaces/where words move." The section *Light and Color* lures you in with the subtlety of the light and color play of the prairie, before forcing you to "think past particles" and embrace color as a tangible, three-dimensional, solid thing. "Are we breathing color?" the poet asks and, later, talks about "rivers of blue sound" that invite you to "listen with your eyes." The collection, *Loose Ends,* is full of inventive juxtaposition that continually asks the reader to think differently about nature, about time, and about space. And, therefore, about relationships. It is a collection you will want to stay with for awhile, dipping in and out as time and fancy permit, " because there is a pause before arriving-" or finishing. "before finding a pattern." A collection you will want to return to, time and again."

-Joan Hawkins, *School and Suicide,*
The Burroughs Hour

"Brenda Linkeman's *Loose Ends* is like stepping into a Monet painting where colors become concepts and every line is filled with light. With a style best described as "ancient master," each poem is a meditation on an emotion, stripped down to its essence. Her poems, such as "Walking Into Water," "Unspoken," and "Sand Timer," are filled with bare-bone wisdom that gently guide the reader to places of healing and peace.Brenda's poems are part Taoist verse, part Buddhist Koan, and all masterfully written. *Loose Ends* is the book I didn't realize I needed and, much like a beautiful painting, I'll return to again and again."

-Chris Dean Author, Co-Founder of Keeping the Flame Alive Press; Indiana Beat Poet Laureate (2025-2027)

Loose Ends

Poems by Brenda Linkeman

Spartan Press

Spartan Press
Kansas City, Missouri
spartanpress.com

Spartan
Press

Author photo: Brenda Linkeman
Cover painting: Abstract painting by Brenda Linkeman
Title page image: "Frayed" by Brenda Linkeman

Acknowledgments:

The author would like to thank the editors of the following publications where some of these poems first appeared (in some form or another): "Watch the Moon", in "This Unexpected Life", published by Spartan Press, 2022; "Seasons Changing", in "Birds in Flight," published by Spartan Press, 2024; and "Wild Seeds" in "Wolf at the Door, Nobody Home" *The Gasconade Review,* 2023.

Again, I would like to thank Rebecca Shaffer for letting me stay in her home in Soulard St. Louis while she was away during the winter months. It is a perfect place for fostering creativity, and gave me a quiet place to write.

I would like to thank the following people for providing venues for poetry to be shared in the Ozarks: John Dorsey for bringing poets in from all over the country to the Osage Arts Community (OAC) in Belle, MO, and hosting Open Mic; Agnes Vojta for organizing and hosting readings and Open Mic at "Poetry at the Pub" in Rolla, MO; and, Loretta Peterman, President of Arts Rolla for her continuing support of poetry through the yearly April "Poet Speak" event, and the biennial writing contest.

I am grateful to my family supporters, as well as the encouragement I get from my friends and Facebook followers.

As always, I am very appreciative for the continuing support of the Osage Arts Community, and in particular for Mark McClane, who first encouraged me to publish.

Table of Contents:

Light and Color

Round Emotions

Time and Moon

Paths

Loose Ends is a collection of work that spans the paths and stages of my life. The ageless themes of– color – time – light – emotion –are woven into all conscious   experiences, and together, offer a deeper and broader understanding of life.

-Brenda Linkeman

This collection of poems is dedicated to my two nieces, Emma Linkeman and Molly Linkeman – Adams. These intelligent and fun-loving sisters have brought a lot of joy into my life as their aunt. Both young women have a talent for writing, and my hope is that they will continue to write, and will share their words often.

LIGHT
AND
COLOR

LILACS AND YELLOW SAFFRON

lilacs and yellow saffron
spread their transference
into molecules
unlike temperance
as roots emerge
in place of trunks
- and leaves
- and transplants
patience and sweet mangos
- waste lands
- and coal
meant for vines
and jungles
replaced
with pale lizards
and multi-colored parrots
still vibrant with color
and personality

WALKING INTO WATER

cornflowers
shimmer
and come together
in a cool stream
torn pieces of
water-soaked oak
and redbud
golden burnished leaves
float and converge
because the time will come
when walking into water
will not be absurd

ITS OWN DOME

blue creates
its own dome
in this blue
it's within reach
it's out there
or maybe here
are we breathing color
does the color
impact our cells
our breath
our voice
this blue
that encompasses me
is a calm force

COPPER LACED TREES

copper laced trees
and woody stems
reach for blue azure
reach for the gentle breeze
they fall together
in unison
with help
to spiral down
forming a thicket
a woodland
a shelter
for feathers
for forest bathing
       -sights
       -sounds
       -scents
immersed in senses
connected

MUSICAL LIGHT

vibrations
push through
my thoughts
I have a need
to discover
an error
a pause
a portal
to open
the musical light
that connects the stars

MYSTICAL INSIGHTS

insights remain
connected to mystical ties
of language
hazes
sight
illuminating gray shades
ocean's white sand
moon's blue light
in your soul
remains the same

WARM MIST

warm mist
keeps rolling
while a cacophony
of communication
rises and falls
searching for harmony
in the morning
it will justify
the clear blue
somehow

WILD SEEDS

through golden harvested fields
surviving dusty solitude
between rows and rows of rich soil
farmed and plowed and considered
steps leading beyond light
to open and closed field gates
on and on till gates are left behind
and paths open to large spaces
of flowing dreams
where wild seeds grow
and create the only place
with no need for opinions

FIELDS OF COMPASSION

growth
throwing light
harvesting no contempt
reaping lavender effects
in the seed of life
in the plot
of a spinning world
in fields of compassion

LEMON SUN

this still remembrance
of sensory pieces
and remnants
of a time filled
with lemon sun
green expansion
in a field of waves
strolling
with no hesitation
toward
a river of blue sound

LIZARDS LEAP

lizards leap
to a precipice
the sun completes a cycle
and orange marmalade
covers sundials in the shade
who notices white daisies
and moss-covered chocolate
just a day
and yet
here we are
existing in a vestibule
of dim light
transforming and straining
for full disclosure
extending
the capacity
of natural science
where portals
are actually
larger than fractals

INTENSITIES OF COLORS

clear colored skies
long wavelengths
of red
orange
yellow
shorter wavelengths
of purple
pink
blue
violet
forming undefined borders
enlightening
colorless time

WILD STRAWBERRIES

balance is fleeting
passing quickly
down a row of obscurity
unknown
unclear
difficult to understand
rocky greens
copper lace
sundrenched leaves
reach toward
a lasting sense
of a renewed season
of wild strawberries

LOOSE ENDS

when the sun sets
on a lower presence
immediate decisions occur
thoughts ramble
toward lavender definitions
in many varied directions
gathering clarity
moments
of confusion
deepest regrets
where the past requires
you to make sense
of loose ends
attempts to prevent
the unraveling of pretense
this sunset
welcomes a certain darkness
an invitation
to reflect
consider

LEADING TO A BOLD INCLUSION

cars emerging meeting
at golden stripes
gazing out at grown people
wearing popcorn hats
and strawberry eyes
skeletons attached to antennae
dangling in thin electric air
merging onto lanes
and black top sliding
slipping onto a shiny path
leading to a bold inclusion
where purple ivy tangles messages
that only a skinny image
can ascertain

JOIN THE EARTH

golden green sunlight
catching hearts
whisping in a single breeze
a faint shivering
as copper
and burgundy
and burnt orange
leaves
join the earth

CRISP LINES

crisp lines
surround orange tomatoes
avocado vines
cling to ripe ideas
and the stanza opens
a way of thinking
beyond color and shape
into a horizon of light points
connecting - yet separate
in the fractal spaces
filled with grains
worlds apart
seemingly one – but many
seeds continue the shapes and hues
maybe green
maybe yellow
maybe red
a genetic decision
sometimes mutated
revealing new dimensions

WITH LIGHT

somewhere ahead
in an outlying path
to perfect color
illumination remains
constrained
while improper combinations
of unharmonious living
are uncovered
only in communication
with light

CROWS AND GULLS

shiny black crows
engage the land
       -are smart
       -mate for life
       -have huge brains
       -and make tools
gulls are not as bold
but are divine
they flow through salt air
like tiny sail boats
in water waves
symbolizing
       -light
       -peace
       -purity
       -clarity

ROUND
EMOTIONS

THIN LINE

empty drains
full saturation
of speed and sound
a thin line
balances a veil
a thread
one tone
empty
but in saturation
you sense
what is left

PAUSE

there is a pause before deciding
a pause before change
change alluding the persistent past
change moving forward to gain perspective
continual step after step toward a place
that shrouds missteps and misadventures
lost in the spaces between time and sound
continual movement and flow
absorbing friction and vibration
there is a pause before the destination
there is a pause before arriving
before finding a pattern
before accepting the past as a foundation

IT MATTERS

listen with your eyes
it matters how we process this
this carousel of relevance
circling with concerns that disturb
that are underfoot and overhead
in actions where dirt and rocks
have smothered terror
and elements
of dark, rolling thunder
obscure a complete vision
where cries and reasoning overlap
but don't meet in the middle
listen with your eyes
there is a circle of innocence
a circle of uncertainty
a dark, dark circle of the unimaginable
notice the overlapping circles
solutions lie in the overlap
it has to be

CLIFF'S EDGE

trails lead to a space
not defined by
any sensory experience
temporary markers
define the boundaries
and the cliffs edge
remains just outside our reach
it seems close
but just barely

IN THE STILLNESS

in the stillness
of a dew drop
lies no small solution
silence is heavy
in the midst of loss
forward movement
not so new
as solutions lie
in tiny clans or tribes
with their meetings
among a few
who are not lost
and who take new interest
in a view of lives
spent understanding ties
and connections
and a lasting past
in the quiet
sudden refreshing
that changes in rhythm
and quenches life

ROUND EMOTIONS

emotions
circle
touch and
connect
like a merry-go-round
of circumference
the center
bursting with
round emotions
of harmony
unity
inclusivity
because
symmetry
lacks hard edges

TOES JUMPED

in the strong
mountain breeze
their hair
and fabric
and rivers
joined in festivity
bones and tones
toes and legs
jumped and played
and leaped for joy
the energy was pure
the life was theirs

UNSPOKEN

we don't know each other
in the city
only what we observe
and draw on from
our life experience
I don't know yours
and you don't know mine
so we search for clues
expressions
our shoes
our pockets
is there a phone
a wallet
maybe a gun
how we walk
there is something
unspoken

SOUNDS ARE STORED

trauma takes many forms
visual trauma imprints the brain
sounds are stored
even smells
repeated trauma can be hard
challenges with sleep
challenges with people
replace with something positive
every day

     a walk

     a garden

     a flower

     a smile

venture out and reconnect

     reprogram

     reinvest

BAKED CHICKEN

and aahhh helped
and society was shook up
and was dipped
in coatings
of an abundance of decisions
and those children
became aware
of personalities
- and differences
- and conflict
- and indecision
following
little Mikey
- and Shirley
- and Spankey
and the tide rolled on
into a bursting
bloom
of pixels and blue
where eyes
and screens
locked
and forgot all about
baked chicken

FOR ALL THE POETS

appropriate responses
of arrogance and time
is retribution in force
rhymes are captured
music and portraiture too
we delve into healing
for all the indecision
for all the poets
who are
reserved
quiet
and unassuming

WHEEL OF STRIFE

peaceful circumstances
won't prevail
during the push and pull
of an endless wheel of strife
sometimes
there is no end
to the failed attempts
focused on the lull
and competition becomes a life
with no end to prevail
with no end to the outcome

STRONGER THAN REALITY

breaking the cycle
is a challenge
a struggle
a lasting effort
better than games
stronger than reality

HOW WILL WORLDS EXIST

the complicated approach
leaves bare the frosty air
wondering where strength remains
lofty cares of strange beings
generate waves of angry water
monotheistic
yet loveless
how will worlds exist

THE PROBLEM OF DEATH

human life
meant to prepare for death
time is the fundamental feature
of the universe
the basic aspect
of subjective reality
time does not exist outside the universe
outer divisions
and durations
and spans
are manmade
the soul needs contemplation of time
to solve the problem of death
in that respect
time can be the greatest enemy of life

FINALLY

in the cellular places
where feelings compete
with concerns that shouldn't rhyme
where imaginary words
attempt to seep
out of pores
and pretend they can think
on their own
when random papers
caught by breezes
collect in tree hollows
where they collude
and work their way
into some type of meaning
some type of plan
where something
finally makes sense

BROKEN BRANCH

a broken branch
can only support so much
before weight pulls it down
cares beyond a different time
plans made sure and bold
life protects
no wind allures
instincts intact
create a bond
a place
you can endure

TECHNICAL EMOTIONS

generations
flow together
seamlessly
until they don't
plows to soil
cylinders to steel
blue screen to chips
crossing the threshold
carrying genetics
and mitochondria
vaccinating against fears
protection beyond doubt
the interface
needing contemplation
- eye
- hair
- skin
other qualities persist
- soil
- faith
- steel
- determination
- curiosity
creating technical emotions

TIME
AND
MOON

EXISTENCE

long after moon floated
and distance destroyed light
lost in a trail of
illumination
into a space of focused sight
traveling fast
traveling on a path
that leads beyond
blackness
beyond destinations
time has no depth
depth has no meaning
layer after layer of questions
distance is confusing
the concept is not new
existence can be renewed

PARTICLES

think past particles
and fractal spaces
where words move
words made of letters
not numbers
individual pieces
scribed by a mind
– hand
– ink
divisions on and on infinitely
forever split

SPONTANEITY

luminary
an inspiration
from mountains
and the universe
in motion with light
a sight that quiets spirits
by transparency
spontaneity
awareness
a special energy
that is transmitted
shared
portion for portion
an exchange
in the broader sense

MOONS BLUE LIGHT

insights remain
joined to musical ties
of language
illuminating gray shadows
the ocean's white sand
like tiny crystals
and moon's blue light
filling your
multicolored soul

PROGRESS OF EXISTENCE

time
the progress of existence
a measured process
on a non-spatial continuum
when time seems long – we are bored
time measures events or quantity
and all events succeed each other
it is endless when in pain
and slow when we wait
it is a succession from
the past - to the present - to the future
it is linear
it is qualitative
time is a fundamental feature of the universe

EXACT PAIRS

are there ever exact pairs
is there a pair
matching infinity
or greater than a pair
how many numbers
can a human mind contain
numbers can't be the answer
when you finish a list
it dissolves and
time may have been wasted
infinity is infinite
some run into a brick wall
some float through
a changed pattern

TRAINED SECRECY

love missed
the sunset this evening
and settled
into a quiet observance
of trained secrecy
private authority
setting with the sun
as bright titles evaporate
into moon light

LINES

lines cross grey
untouching
taut
trees
still clouds
deep
dense
whisper now
whisper later
and the moon
may shine

VASTNESS OF INSPIRATION

sensitivity is increasing
my perception
the incentive is not hidden
just dormant
as a still pause
in a double standard
I then explore
the vastness of inspiration
illuminated 186,000 miles
into space

SAND TIMER

history is a sand timer
each grain funnels through
at it's appropriate
appointed moment
turned back
at times
to follow
the same course
later

BLIND GEESE

ominous resurgence
secures flights
to eternity for most
star dust settles
on the galaxy
the moon eclipses again
and again
as blind geese
stir slightly

WATCH THE MOON

late night decaf
stirred sweet with a fork
cooled
swirled
and bubbling air
below the surface
no cold steps
just an open window
enough to breathe
and for
cat
to watch the moon

HIDDEN PRINCIPALITIES

continuous vibrations
between towers
and lovers
and receivers
and deceivers
halted by hidden principalities
in unspeakable realms
edged into
endless realms
of star light
and moon light

TUMBLING INTO TIME

tumbling into time
passages colored
a pyramid
of intense color
blue to orange
yellow to purple
red to green
white to black
space lacks substance

NO CHANGE NO TIME

time –
the result of fluctuations of sensations
drugs and neurotransmitters
can affect the perception of time
it is dependent on sensations
in trauma and emergencies time slows down
the amygdala is active and super-charged
multiple memories are being formed
and during long periods of inactivity
with little stimulation between successive events
the amygdala is slow
and time seems to go faster
when there is no change
there is no time

SEASONS CHANGING

seasons relegate their days
with sun and moon
but further on
no light remains
no star
no frost
no wind
months begin to fade
a bird speeds fast
river mist lifts
over trees
streams
and even so
cold prevails

PATHS

POWER OF RAIN

yet in all the possible places
information was drastic
yet lately mistaken
there was
a line
a course
a task
to rise above
the power of rain
and dwell among the race
of inconsistency and trust
in place of distant days
as to remembrances listed
opportunities forgotten
in vague
misplaced rhymes

LITERAL BREEZES

literal breezes escape
in earnest
seeping between
tags and taxes
into bright generations
within reach
cascading toward
stairs and steps
leading beyond expectations
toward
a long descent
beneath pressure
and steam
force and push
a stronger wind –
is it destructive
or is it healing

SILENT CRIES

in the dark
travelling through caves
obscured by silent cries
the sky floats
soil is deep
they form a pact
and blend to
decide the future
before sailing
toward harmony
and tranquility

LOST IN YEARS

I reach for fears
so fine a thread
that weaves a web
searching unveils truth
yet conceals the vines
that cling inside my head
I reach for fears
just out of grasp
lines lost in years
mirrors
that eventually expose
traces of losses
faint traces
nevertheless

DISORDER CAN CEASE

too tense

too mirrored

these vowels

I wring the meanings out

alarm

calm

blameless

climbing

soaring

sky high

explanations are dreary

yet disorder can cease

in these lines

in these times

SYLLABLES THAT SHOUT

I want to write about

feelings

emotions

raw anger

insides turning out

shoulders back

pride

revenge

terror

words and definitions

syllables that shout

more than chapters

with beginnings that end

more than brief temperate tension

SOME DAYS

some days are puzzling
with no regrets
just being in the moment
the second
the hour
beyond the sky
and into cool water
leading to a cascade
of life and growth
and future tests

PATHS

(this is a version of the first poem, a sonnet, that I wrote as a sophomore in high school in Herndon, Virginia)

paths lead in and out of trees
near nesting birds
and playful sounds
hot sun rays stream low
warm winds blow
in gusts and heaves
you turn
around and 'round and 'round
no shelter to be seen
the rain keeps pouring
down and down
so you begin to flee
you pause and turn
and understand
that storms aren't seen
through your closed eyes
you learn it takes space
to know there is peace
it takes time

DOES IT MATTER

history in syllables
and consonants
typed and stored
boxed and taped
and shredded
like evidence lost
to the future
marking time no more
receipts showing
when and where
you were for days and weeks
marking your place
does it matter

LETTER BY LETTER

I searched for words
the thoughts I bore
made refuse cheap
troubled minds
delved into
page by page
syllable by syllable
letter by letter
word by word

FLOW THROUGH MY SOUL

start over
begin with insight
and empathy for life
plants and trees
are very personal
and rustle lightly
in the circling breezes
with water and streams
flowing through my soul
strengthening my core
to a strong conclusion

BEYOND THE PEAK

climbing mountains
reaching for cliffs
crevices
touching
a certain space
beyond the peak
beyond reach

SPLASHES

congregating
around a fountain
with no depth
just splashes
and his reflection

SIGNS

persistent displeasure
time passes
time and time again
systems consign
banish
place
rank
condition
was something assumed
I stumble with tolerance
mask out signs
to keep the peace
is it as necessary
as you think

Brenda Linkeman is a poet, artist, and child therapist, known for her poetry collections "This Unexpected Life" (2022), and "Birds in Flight" (2024), both published by Spartan Press. She has also published poems in literary journals like *The Gasconade Review, Trailer Park Quarterly,* and *Literary Revelations Press.* Her work is inspired by people, the universe, and observations of nature, particularly birds, and the health of the planet. Brenda regularly participates in local poetry readings and open mic events.

This project was made possible, in part, by generous support from the Osage Arts Community.

Osage Arts Community provides temporary time, space and support for the creation of new artistic works in a retreat format, serving creative people of all kinds — visual artists, composers, poets, fiction and nonfiction writers. Located on a 152-acre farm in an isolated rural mountainside setting in Central Missouri and bordered by ¾ of a mile of the Gasconade River, OAC provides residencies to those working alone, as well as welcoming collaborative teams, offering living space and workspace in a country environment to emerging and mid-career artists. For more information, visit us at www.osageac.org

Osage Arts Community